REGIONS OF THE UNITED STATES

EXPLORE NEW ENGLAND

by Kristine Spanier, MLIS

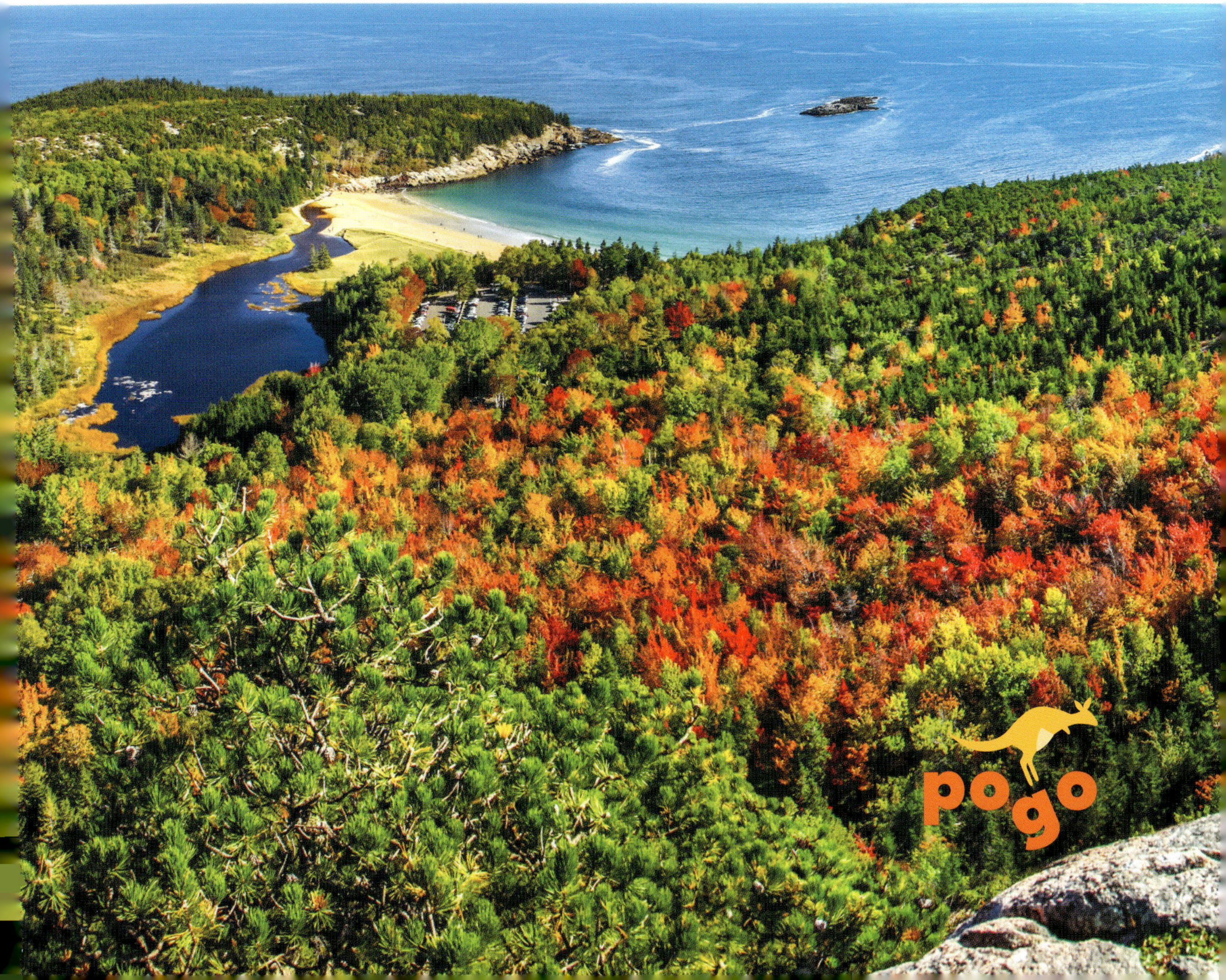

pogo

Ideas for Parents and Teachers

Pogo Books let children practice reading informational text while introducing them to nonfiction features such as headings, labels, sidebars, maps, and diagrams, as well as a table of contents, glossary, and index.

Carefully leveled text with a strong photo match offers early fluent readers the support they need to succeed.

Before Reading

- "Walk" through the book and point out the various nonfiction features. Ask the student what purpose each feature serves.
- Look at the glossary together. Read and discuss the words.

Read the Book

- Have the child read the book independently.
- Invite him or her to list questions that arise from reading.

After Reading

- Discuss the child's questions. Talk about how he or she might find answers to those questions.
- Prompt the child to think more. Ask: In fall, leaves turn colors in New England. Do the leaves change color where you live?

Pogo Books are published by Jump!
5357 Penn Avenue South
Minneapolis, MN 55419
www.jumplibrary.com

Copyright © 2023 Jump! International copyright reserved in all countries. No part of this book may be reproduced in any form without written permission from the publisher.

Library of Congress Cataloging-in-Publication Data

Names: Spanier, Kristine, author.
Title: Explore New England / by Kristine Spanier.
Description: Minneapolis, MN: Jump!, Inc., [2023]
Series: Regions of the United States
Audience: Ages 7-10
Identifiers: LCCN 2021053849 (print)
LCCN 2021053850 (ebook)
ISBN 9781636907208 (hardcover)
ISBN 9781636907215 (paperback)
ISBN 9781636907222 (ebook)
Subjects: LCSH: New England—Juvenile literature.
Classification: LCC F4.3 .S63 2023 (print)
LCC F4.3 (ebook) | DDC 974—dc23/eng/20211202
LC record available at https://lccn.loc.gov/2021053849
LC ebook record available at https://lccn.loc.gov/2021053850

Editor: Jenna Gleisner
Designer: Molly Ballanger

Photo Credits: pisaphotography/Shutterstock, cover (top); haveseen/Shutterstock, cover (middle); Christian Delbert/Shutterstock, cover (bottom); Jason Busa/Shutterstock, 1; Eric Isselee/Shutterstock, 3; Harold M. Lambert/Getty, 4; Stock Montage/Getty, 5; Universal Images Group/SuperStock, 6-7; Don Mennig/Alamy, 8; Mihai_Andritoiu/Shutterstock, 9; Shutterstock, 10-11t, 20-21br; DenisTangneyJr/iStock, 10-11b, 20-21bl; KeithSzafranksi/iStock, 12-13tl; smcarter/iStock, 12-13tr; Joshua Serrano Crisosto/Shutterstock, 12-13bl; Chris Alcock/Shutterstock, 12-13br; traveler1116/iStock, 14; Maxim Gorishniak/Shutterstock, 15; KenWiedemann/iStock, 16-17; Mark Agnor/Shutterstock, 18-19; Stephen Albert Clarke/Shutterstock, 20-21tl; Allan Wood Photography/Shutterstock, 20-21tr; Sean Pavone/Shutterstock, 22t; jtyler/iStock, 22m; Richard Semik/Shutterstock, 22b; Marcio Jose Bastos Silva/Shutterstock, 23.

Printed in the United States of America at Corporate Graphics in North Mankato, Minnesota.

Title Page Image: Acadia National Park, Maine

TABLE OF CONTENTS

CHAPTER 1
History and Location 4

CHAPTER 2
Geography and Wildlife 8

CHAPTER 3
Daily Life 14

QUICK FACTS & TOOLS
Quick Facts 22
Glossary 23
Index 24
To Learn More 24

CHAPTER 1
HISTORY AND LOCATION

In 1620, 102 passengers sailed on the *Mayflower*. They landed in what is now the northeastern United States. These **colonists** were from England. They are known as **Pilgrims**.

By 1641, 20,000 more had arrived. **Indigenous** people already lived here. They helped the colonists. They traded goods with them. But colonists soon wanted more land. They took it. Wars broke out.

CHAPTER 1 | 5

The British government made the colonists pay **taxes**. Colonists wanted **independence**. This started the Revolutionary War (1775–1783). The first two battles took place in Massachusetts. The colonists won the war. The colonies became states. Six of these states make up the **region** that is New England.

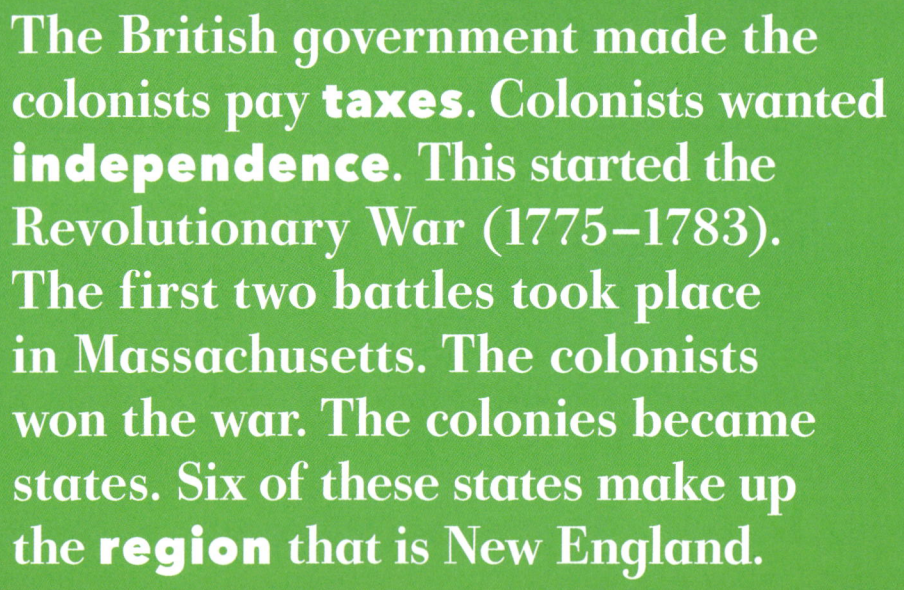

Battle of Lexington

CHAPTER 1

TAKE A LOOK!

Which states are part of New England? Take a look!

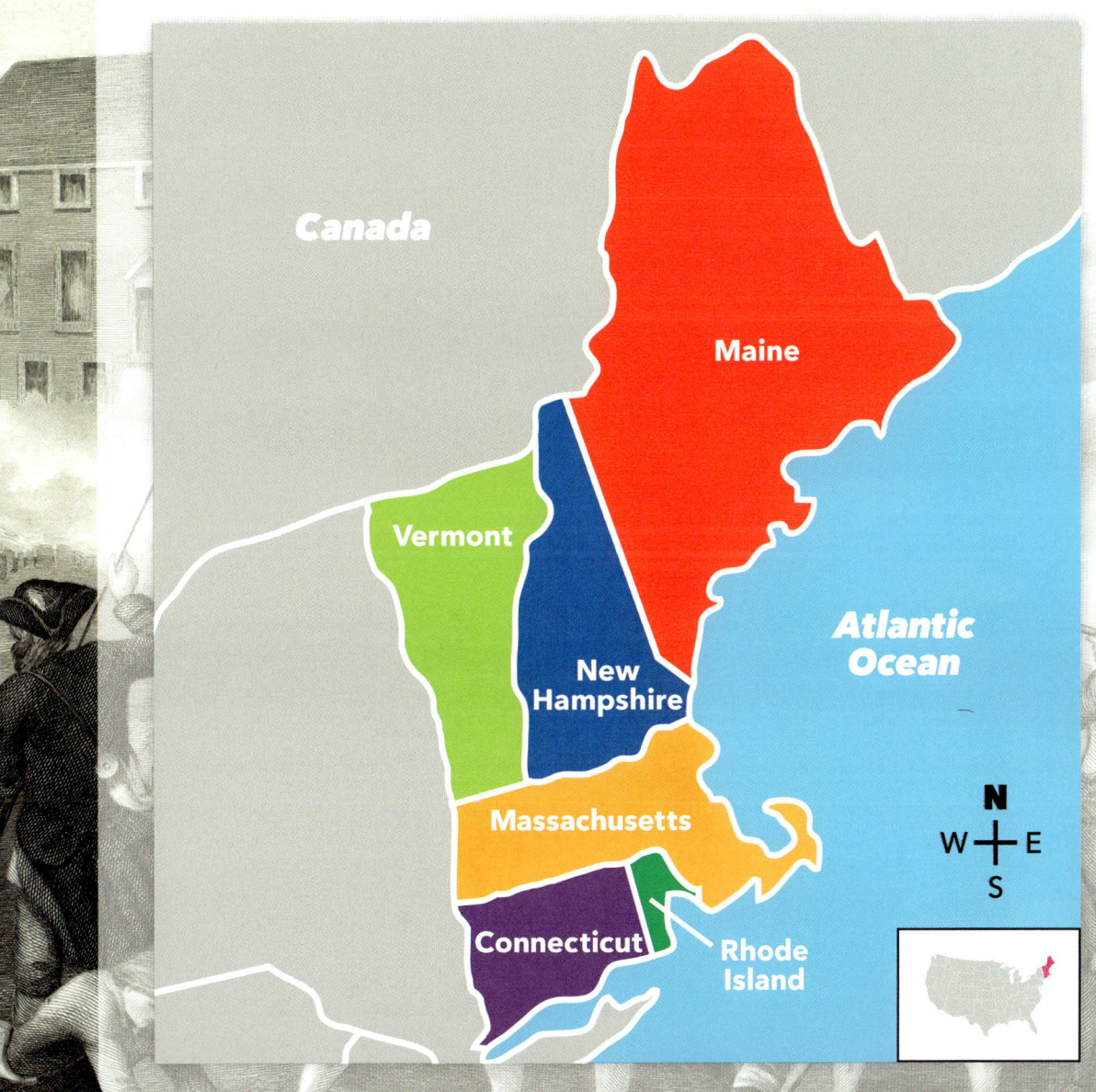

CHAPTER 1　7

CHAPTER 2
GEOGRAPHY AND WILDLIFE

Some of the smallest states in the country are in New England. Rhode Island is the smallest. Narragansett Bay is an **estuary** here. It has more than 30 islands. A single house sits on one island.

Clingstone

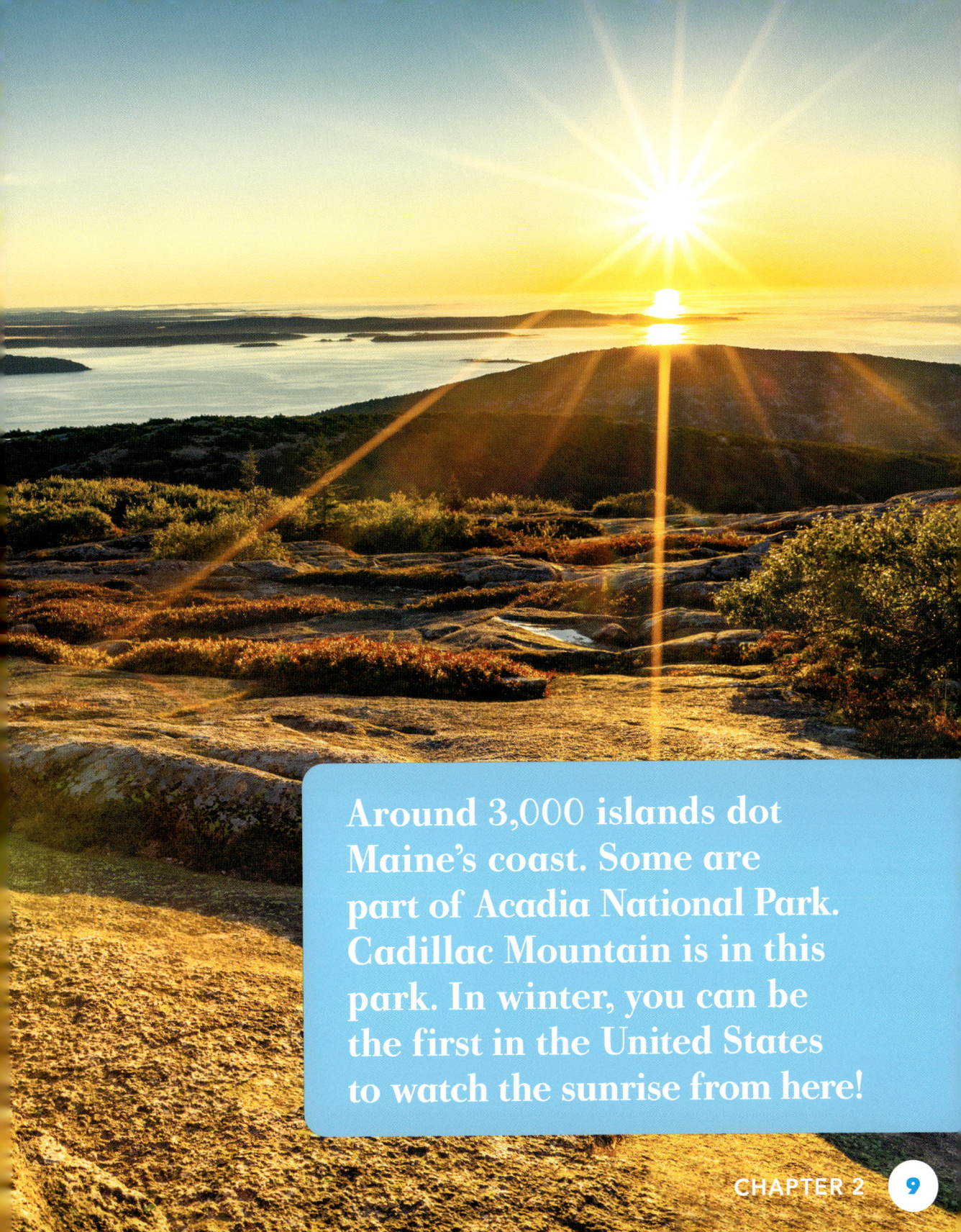

Around 3,000 islands dot Maine's coast. Some are part of Acadia National Park. Cadillac Mountain is in this park. In winter, you can be the first in the United States to watch the sunrise from here!

The White Mountains are in New Hampshire and Maine. Mount Washington is part of this range. At 6,288 feet (1,917 meters) tall, it is the region's highest peak.

The Green Mountains are in Vermont. Maple trees cover them.

CHAPTER 2

Mount Washington

Green Mountains

CHAPTER 2

moose

bobcat

humpback whale

puffins

12 CHAPTER 2

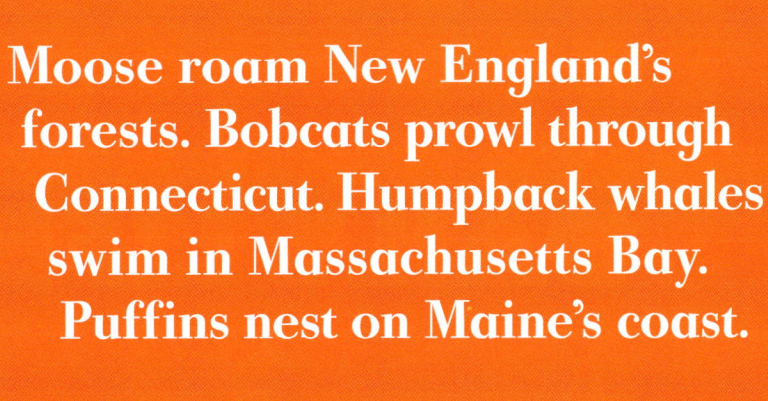

Moose roam New England's forests. Bobcats prowl through Connecticut. Humpback whales swim in Massachusetts Bay. Puffins nest on Maine's coast.

DID YOU KNOW?

Moose antlers are big! They can spread six feet (1.8 m) from end to end.

CHAPTER 2 — 13

CHAPTER 3
DAILY LIFE

Portland Head Light

Would you like to see the oldest lighthouse in Maine? Portland Head Light has been guiding ships since 1791.

Boston, Massachusetts, is the region's most **populated** city. Boston Common is the oldest city park in the country. People ice-skate here in winter!

CHAPTER 3 | 15

New England's **natural resources** provide many jobs. Massachusetts is known for cranberries. Maine is one of the largest **producers** of blueberries. People fish for lobsters, clams, and fish in the Atlantic Ocean. Trees are turned into paper and wood products.

WHAT DO YOU THINK?

Some of Massachusetts's cranberry plants are more than 150 years old! Do you know what plants grow near you? Are any eaten as food?

Many people here work in **manufacturing**. Helicopters and submarines are made in New England. Computers and other electronics are made here, too.

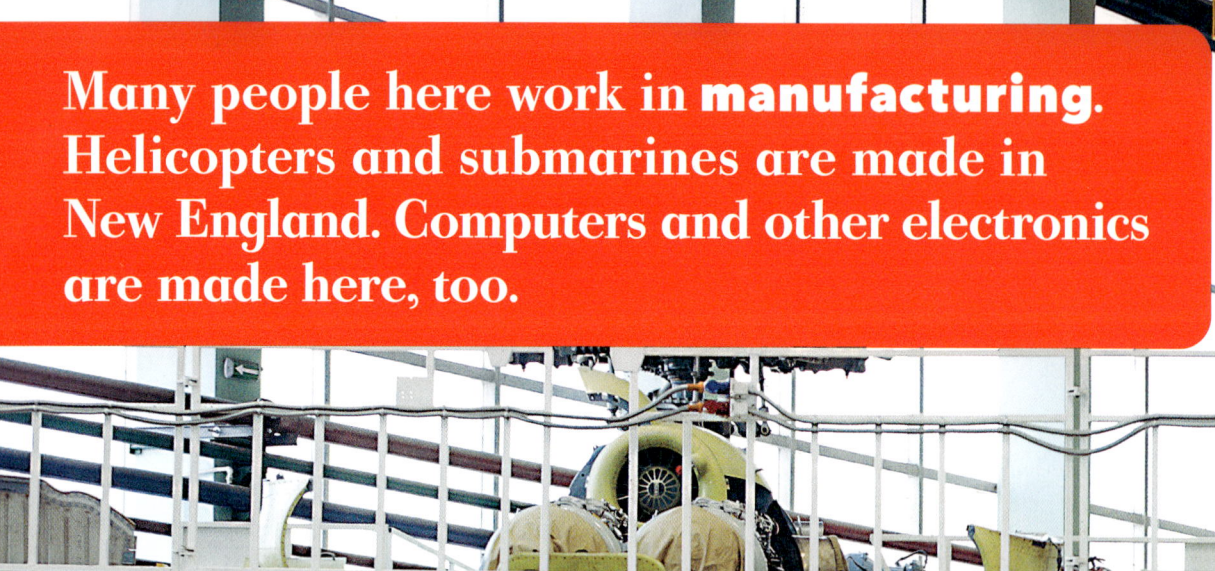

helicopter

TAKE A LOOK!

What are some of New England's top **industries**? Take a look!

Connecticut	Maine	Massachusetts
farming, insurance and business, manufacturing	farming, fishing, tourism, wood products	technology, manufacturing, publishing

New Hampshire	Rhode Island	Vermont
manufacturing, wood products	health care, fishing, tourism	farming, technology, publishing, tourism

= farming   = fishing   = health care

= insurance and business   = manufacturing   = publishing

= technology   = tourism   = wood products

CHAPTER 3   19

spring

summer

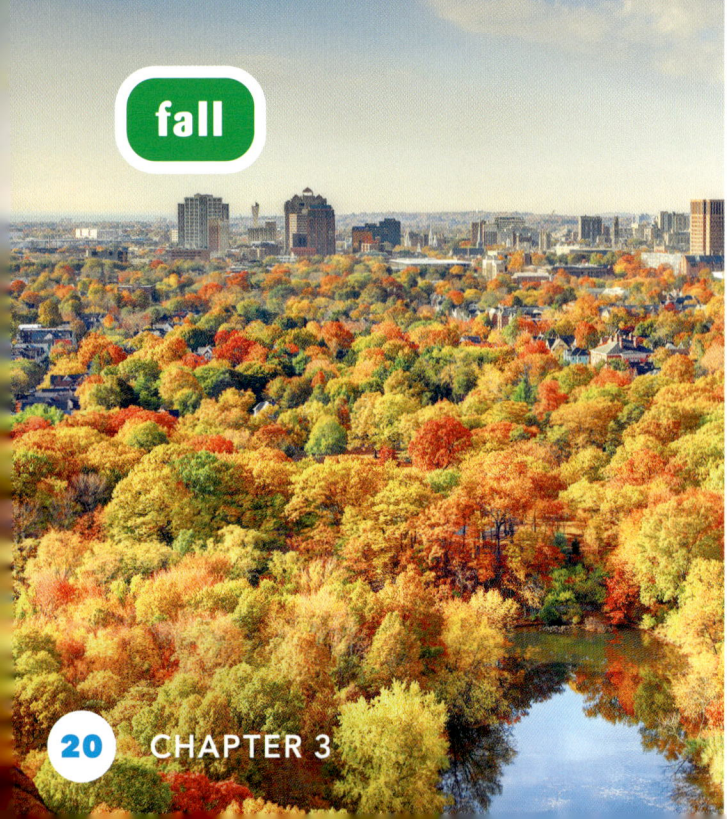
fall

winter

20 CHAPTER 3

New England's weather changes each season. In spring, people collect sap from maple trees to make syrup. People sail off the coast of Cape Cod in summer. Travelers come to see New England's bright fall leaves. When the snow flies, many ski in the mountains!

Have you been to New England? Would you like to go?

WHAT DO YOU THINK?

Vermont produces more maple syrup than any other state. Do you know what your state produces?

CHAPTER 3   21

QUICK FACTS

NEW ENGLAND REGION

Location: northeastern United States

Population (2021 estimate): 15,092,739

Most Populated City in Each State:
Bridgeport, CT
Portland, ME
Boston, MA
Manchester, NH
Providence, RI
Burlington, VT

Top Industries: manufacturing, food production, tourism, insurance and business

Average High Temperature: up to 85 degrees Fahrenheit (29 degrees Celsius)

Average Low Temperature: around 15 degrees Fahrenheit (–9 degrees Celsius)

Major Landforms: Appalachian Mountains, Green Mountains, White Mountains, Taconic Mountains

Highest Point: Mount Washington, NH, 6,288 feet (1,917 m)

Major Waterways: Lake Champlain, Connecticut River, Hudson River, Narragansett Bay, Atlantic Ocean

Major Landmarks: Acadia National Park, Plymouth Rock, Portland Head Light, Boston Common

MANCHESTER, NH

LAKE CHAMPLAIN, VT

ACADIA NATIONAL PARK, ME

GLOSSARY

colonists: People who leave one area to settle in another.

estuary: The wide part of a river, where it joins the ocean.

independence: Freedom from a controlling authority.

Indigenous: Of or relating to the earliest known people to live in a place.

industries: Businesses or trades.

manufacturing: The industry of making something on a large scale using special equipment or machinery.

natural resources: Materials produced by Earth that are necessary or useful to people.

Pilgrims: The group of people who left England because of religious persecution, came to North America, and founded a colony in 1620.

populated: Having people living in it.

producers: People, places, or regions that grow agricultural products or manufacture natural resources into objects humans can use.

region: A general area or a specific district or territory.

taxes: Money that people and businesses must pay in order to support a government.

Plymouth Rock, Massachusetts

QUICK FACTS & TOOLS

INDEX

Acadia National Park 9
animals 13
Boston Common 15
Cadillac Mountain 9
Cape Cod 21
colonists 4, 5, 6
Connecticut 7, 13, 19
Green Mountains 10
Indigenous people 5
industries 18, 19
Maine 7, 9, 10, 13, 14, 16, 19
maple trees 10, 21
Massachusetts 6, 7, 15, 16, 19
Massachusetts Bay 13
Mayflower 4
Mount Washington 10
Narragansett Bay 8
natural resources 16
New Hampshire 7, 10, 19
Pilgrims 4
Portland Head Light 14
Revolutionary War 6
Rhode Island 7, 8, 19
seasons 9, 15, 21
Vermont 7, 10, 19, 21
White Mountains 10

TO LEARN MORE

Finding more information is as easy as 1, 2, 3.

❶ Go to www.factsurfer.com
❷ Enter "exploreNewEngland" into the search box.
❸ Choose your book to see a list of websites.